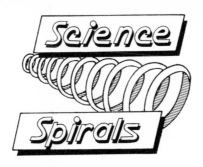

On the Water

Julie Fitzpatrick
Illustrated by Sara Silcock

Silver Burdett Company
Morristown, New Jersey

Library of Congress Cataloging in Publication Data

Fitzpatrick, Julie.
   On the water.

   (Science spirals)
   Includes index.
   Summary: Experiments to demonstrate how and why
cetain things float while others sink, how to load
boats so they don't sink, how to make things float
that might not, and how to bring things up from
underwater.
      1. Floating bodies — Experiments — Juvenile literature.
2. Water — Experiments — Juvenile literature.
[1. Floating bodies — Experiments. 2. Water —
Experiments. 3. Experiments] I. Silcock, Sara, ill.
II. Title.
QC147.5.F58   1985   532′.2′078   84-40836
ISBN 0-382-09058-6

First published in Great Britain in 1984 by
Hamish Hamilton Children's Books
Garden House, 57-59 Long Acre, London WC2E 9J2

Designed by Linda Rogers Associates

Adapted and published in the United States, 1985, by
Silver Burdett Company, Morristown, N.J.

ISBN 0-382-09058-6

Library of Congress Catalog Card No. 84-40836

Introduction

Have you ever wondered why some things come floating in on waves at the seashore and other things never float? Have you wondered how heavy steel ships manage to stay on the top of the water even when they are loaded?

This book is filled with experiments to show you how and why certain things float while others sink. You will learn how to load boats so they don't sink, how to make things float that might not, and how to bring things up from the bottom.

Equipment you need for experiments in this book

Paper
Cardboard
Pencil
Ruler
Scissors
Sticky tape
Clay
An aquarium (called a tank)
   or a bowl of water
A towel
Stones, corks, milk bottle
   tops, a piece of sponge, a
   piece of cloth, shells
Balls
Balloons
House bricks
Plastic trays and tiles
Sticks
A length of rubber tubing
Salt
Egg carton
Match boxes
Aluminum foil

On the Water

Put a cork and a stone in
a tank of water.
What happens to them?

The stone goes down through
the water.
It sinks to the bottom of
the tank.
The cork does not go down.
It floats on top of the water.

What other things can you
find that will float?

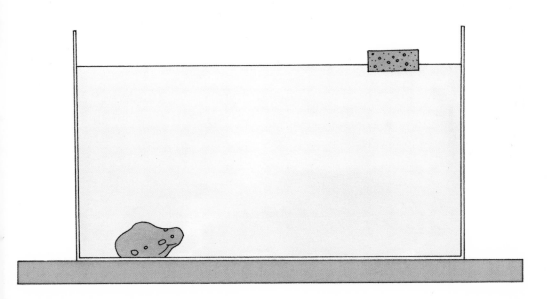

Collect some of these things.
Try each one on the water.
Which things float?

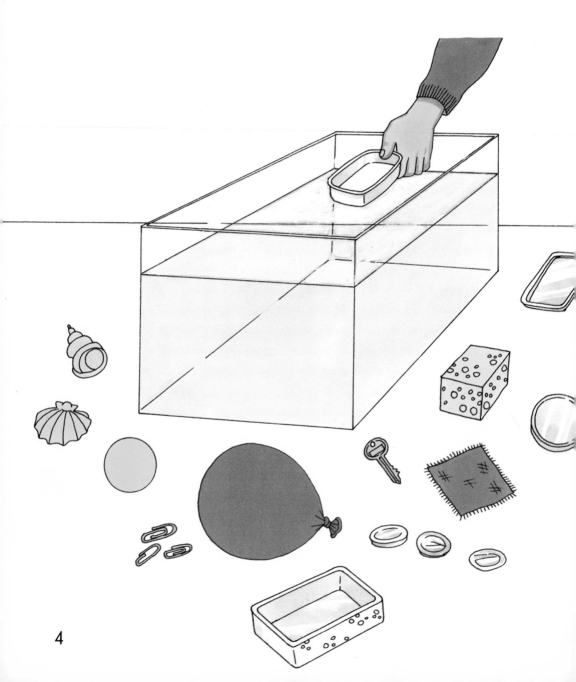

4

Now collect these things.

Copy the chart below onto
a piece of paper.
Draw a picture of the things
down one side of the chart.
Look at each thing and guess
if it will float or sink.
Put a check in one box to show
what you think will happen.
Test each thing to see if
you were right.
Did you have any surprises?
Now put checks in the next boxes
to show what did happen
to each thing.

What do you think will happen?			What did happen?	
Draw here	float	sink	floated	sank

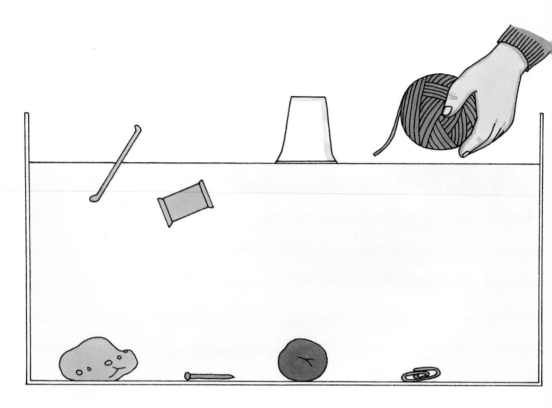

Does it matter which way
you put things on the water?
Try putting a jar lid in
sideways.
Does it still float?
What happens if you put a
plastic cup in upside down?

Leave all the things in the
tank of water.
What do you notice about a
ball of wool if it is left in
the water for a whole day?

The top of the water
is called the surface.
Get an orange and
put it on the surface.
Does most of the orange float above
or below the surface?

Look for some other things
which float below the surface.
Draw the tank of water and
show where the things float.
Which things float on the
surface?
What is different about these
things and the things that float
below the surface?

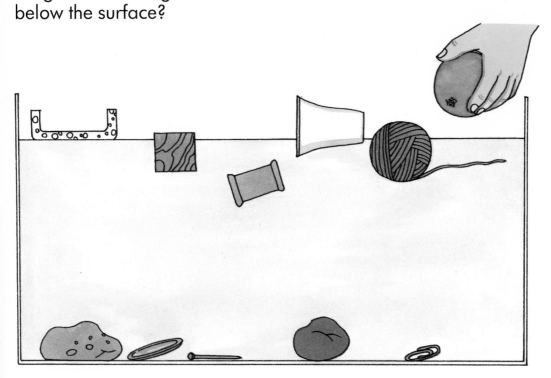

Can you sink the things that
float?
Push the floaters down through
the water.
Which things stay at the bottom?

What happens when you push a
ball or a balloon down?
(They keep coming up to the surface.)

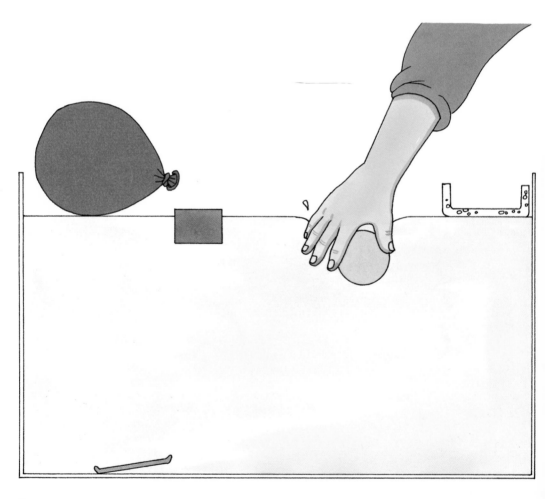

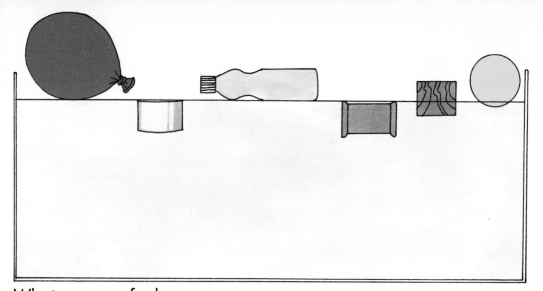

What can you feel as you
push the floaters down through
the water?
You can feel the water pushing
against them.
Do any of the things which
floated on the surface now
float below it?

Make another drawing of the tank.
Show what happened to the
floaters when you tried to
sink them.

Look at the things which
come back up to float on
the surface.
Are they flat?
What are they made of?
Are they round?
What do you think there is
inside of them.

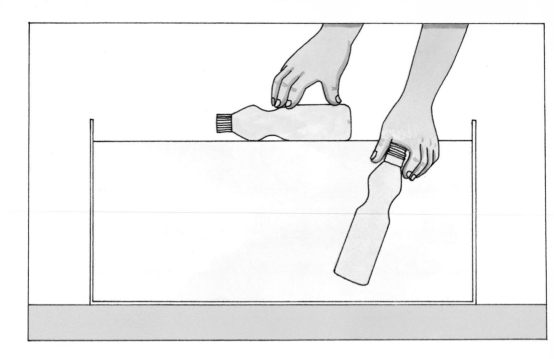

Take all the things out of
the tank and dry them with
a towel.
Get the shampoo bottle and
put it back on the water.
What would you have to do
to make it sink?
Try taking the cap off.
Now push the bottle
down through the water.
The water rushes into
the bottle.
What can you see coming out
of the bottle?
What happens to the bottle
when it is full of water?

When you started, the bottle
looked empty but there was
air inside it.
The water went into the bottle
and pushed the air out.
How could you use a tube to
get air back into the bottle?

Put one end of the tube into
the bottle.
Blow air down the tube.
What can you see coming
out of the bottle?
What happens to the bottle as
it becomes full of air again?

The Sunken Treasure Ship

You need a baby's cup that has
two handles.
Get some paper and draw the
two sides of a ship.
Cut them out and stick them
onto the cup.
Make some treasure by wrapping
stones in aluminum foil.
Load the treasure into the ship,
then push it down to the
bottom of the sea.
You need something that floats
to help lift the ship to the
surface.
How could you use ballons
to help?

Blow up two balloons halfway.
Ask an adult to help you fasten
some string around the neck
of each balloon.
You can be the diver who attaches
the balloons to the sunken ship.
Get a friend to help you push
each balloon under the water.
Tie the balloons to the handles
on the side of the ship.
How does the sunken ship
get up to the surface?

Air is used like this to
get real sunken ships back
up to the surface.
Divers fix large bags around
the sunken ship.
Air is pumped into the bags
to help lift the ship.

A hovercraft has a cushion of
air underneath it.
This lifts it up and helps it
glide easily over the water.

When you swim, the air in your
lungs helps you stay up in
the water.
When you are learning to swim,
you can wear arm-bands or a tube.
They are filled with air to
help you float.
People who go sailing can wear
a life jacket.
The jacket has air inside.
If they fall into the water,
the jacket will help them float.

15

Shape a ball of clay so
it fits in the palm of your hand.
What will happen to it in water?
If you change the shape of the
clay, you may get it to float.

Make some of these shapes.
Test each one to see if it floats.
What will happen if there is a hole in your shape?

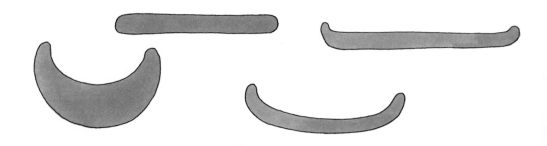

When you have made a shape that
will float, see if it will carry
any cargo.
Gently load the shape with
small coins.
How many coins will it carry?

Can you change the shape to
carry more coins?
Does it help if the bottom
is flatter?
Does it help if the sides
are higher?

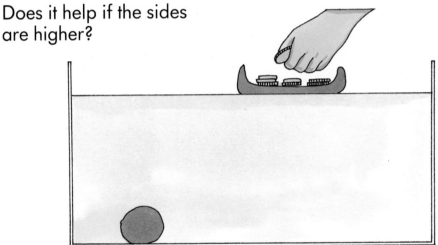

Real ships are made of iron.
You might think that a ship
made of metal would sink.
The metal has to be shaped,
as you have done with the clay.
Then the ship will float and
carry cargo.

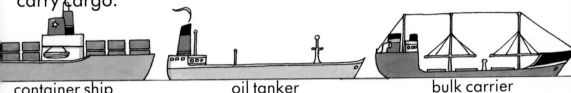

container ship   oil tanker   bulk carrier

Get the bottom part of an
egg carton for the hull of a boat.
Use some small stones as
cargo and load the boat.
What happens to the boat if
you load the cargo all on
one side?
What happens if you load the
heaviest stones at the front?
Which is the best way to
load the cargo so that the
boat does not sink?

Ships have to be loaded
very carefully.
The cargo is stored in containers
so that it cannot move around.
Get some match boxes to use as
the containers.
Fill some with small stones
and others with sand or coins.
This time, use the lid of the
egg carton as the hull.

Which is the best way to
load the ship with the
containers?
What if the cargo of sand was the
first to be taken off the ship?
Where would be the best place
to store this cargo?

19

What happens to the water
when you put things into
the tank?
Get some house bricks.
Carefully put one brick into
the tank.
What do you notice about
the water?

Take the brick out again.
This time mark the level
of the water before the
brick goes in.
Carefully put the brick in again.
Mark the level of the water.
Measure how many inches
the water has risen.
Why does the level of the
water go up?

When you put the brick into the
tank it pushes some water away.
The water cannot go to the
bottom so it comes up around
the sides of the brick.
How far do you think the
water will rise if you put
a second brick into the tank?
Try it and see.

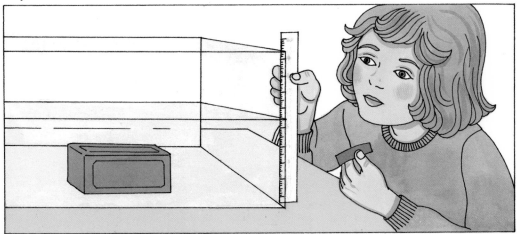

Make a table like this
to show what you find out.

How far did the water rise?	
1 brick	
2 bricks	

The water in the ocean is salty.
You might have tasted it when
you have been in the ocean.
Does it make any difference if
a boat is floating in fresh
river water or salty ocean water?

This is how you can find out.
Get two plastic pots and
put the same amount of water
in each one.
Stir two cups of salt into
one of the pots.

Make a boat that will fit into
the pots.
Load the boat with cargo.
Put it into each pot in turn.
Mark the level of the water
on the side of the boat each time.
What do you notice?
Does the boat float higher in
fresh water or salty water?

Fresh

Salty

Things float better in salty water.
They do not sink so far into it.
If a ship is in salty water
it floats higher than if
it is in fresh water.
Would a ship be able to carry more
cargo in salty water or fresh water?

Put your boat in salty water.
Load it with cargo, but do not
sink it.
Lift the boat out of the salty
water and put it in fresh water.
What happens to it?

The boat could carry more cargo
in salty water because it floats
higher than in fresh water.
Every ship has a mark on the
side to show how deep it must float
when it is loaded.
This mark is called the Plimsoll line.
What would happen to ships
if they were loaded with
too much cargo?

These marks
are for ships
in fresh
water

These marks
are for ships
in salt
water

How to make your own Sail Boat

Look at the things which floated.
Choose one that you think would
make a good hull for a sail boat.

You need ★ a stick for the mast
            ★ some cardboard to make the sail
            ★ clay

You need to draw and
cut out a sail.
Think what shape the sail could be.
How big does it need to be
to catch the wind and
move the boat along?
How tall will the mast be?
Thread the sail onto the mast.

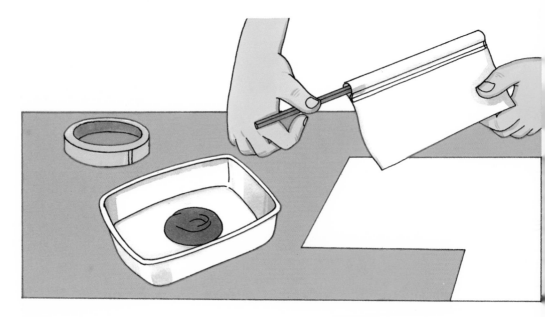

Where is the best place to
put the mast?
Use a blob of clay to
fix the mast to the hull of
the boat.
Test your sail boat on
the water.
If the boat tips over, there
may be something wrong with
the size of the sail or the mast.

See how you can change them
to make the boat float.
Blow into the sail of the boat
to make it move on the water.
How far does it sail?
What can you do to make
it change direction?

Start collecting pictures of
things that move on the water.
What do you know about any
of these things.

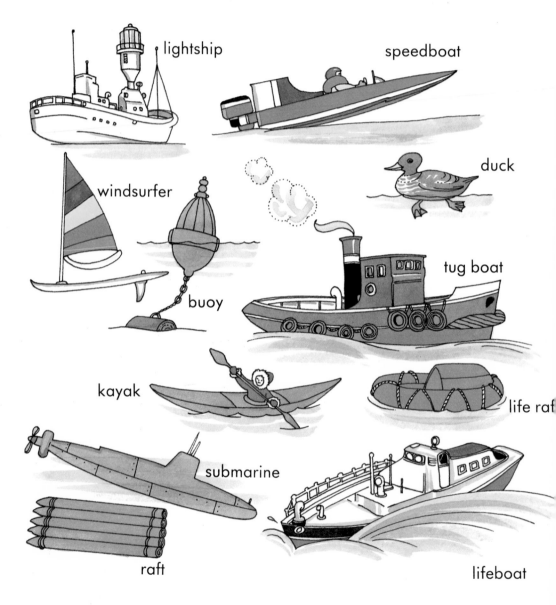

lightship

speedboat

windsurfer

duck

buoy

tug boat

kayak

life raft

submarine

raft

lifeboat

How to play Think or Sink

Get a box and put these things inside.

What could happen to these things in water?
Make cards like this.

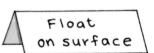

Float on surface

Ask a friend to put his or her hand into the box and take out one of the things.
What does your friend think will happen to it in water?
Test it and put it by the right card.
Do the same with the other things in the box.
Work out some more things to make your friends think—
or sink!

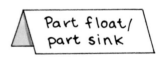

Part float/ part sink

Sink

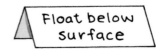

Float below surface

Index

Notes for parents and teachers

Floating and sinking work is best done in a plastic or glass aquarium. Children can then see the items from the side, at their eye level.
The chart on page 5 represents one way of recording which things float and which things sink. You may like to have duplicated sheets of this chart ready to fill in.

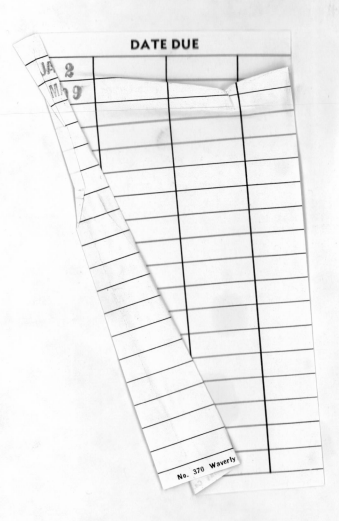

DATE DUE

JA 2

MR 9

No. 370 Waverly